Allgemeine Entwurfsanstalt with Trix and Robert Haussmann
Furniture for Röthlisberger Kollektion

With contributions by:
Peter Röthlisberger
Alfred Hablützel
Trix and Robert Haussmann

Niggli

Contents

Preface

First Encounters with Robert Haussmann

I was a small boy of seven. My father made his first contacts with Teo Jakob, whom he met through his friend Hans "Jöggu" Eichenberger. Eichenberger and my father knew each other from sports. Both at the time worked for the prestigious Bern company Jörns, which produced furniture and interior installations.

Hans Eichenberger later had a studio in Bern's historic quarter, three doors down from Teo Jakob. After my father took over the family business, our carpenter's workshop, together with Eichenberger, manufactured furniture and interior fixtures. Through his contact with Jöggu and Teo, my father then met Robert Haussmann.

Between 1959 and 1962, Hans Eichenberger designed the furniture series HE 153, which we manufactured and then marketed through Teo Jakob and later also through Wohnbedarf Zurich and Basel. At that time the furniture landscape looked very different: except for Knoll International, there were no furniture collections; a brand-name furniture collection was as yet unknown. Furniture dealers sold their own fabricated products, and buyers were not meant to know who made them.

As of 1958, we built Knoll International prototypes and began producing furniture for the Knoll collection. I learned of names like Florence Knoll, Marcel Breuer, Mies van der Rohe, Harry Bertoia, Richard Schulz, George Nelson, Charles Eames, Eero Saarinen and many others. As a small boy I naturally never realized what these names meant. I couldn't differentiate between design and fabrication, because from our workshop I only knew of fabrication. These names gradually took on shape; I became interested in the people behind the names, and above all in their work, though I didn't realize that they would accompany me my whole life long.

Knoll International was sold through Wohnbedarf Zurich; Ueli Wieser and Koni Ochsner were responsible for the Swiss Knoll design. It was a furniture collection adapted to Swiss needs.

It was at this time that I met Robert Haussmann. My father spoke of "Herr Haussmann", Teo Jakob's friend, who came from big, far-off Zurich. I remember very well the first time that this distinguished gentleman from Zurich came to visit us. He drove up in an impressive automobile, wore a fine hat and a handsome suit. Not till much later was it clear to me that the automobile was a Bentley. I don't know what impressed me most about Robert Haussmann. Was it the car, was it the fine hats and suits, the foreign language (the Zurich Swiss dialect was a foreign language to a child from Bern), or the combination of all three? Quite certainly I was impressed by the precise lines he set down in his drawings. Robert had the talent and the skill to sketch realistic drawings, quickly and exactly.

Between 1960 and 1975 we manufactured specially designed furniture and interior installations for and with Robert Haussmann. Our first piece of furniture by Robert that was sold in specialist shops was a no-frills sofa table with a top of opaque glass. This table was sold by the same specialist traders as the HE 153 furniture series. I especially remember the early interior decoration he did for an IBM shop in Bern. The shop's room was very small and Robert, with mirrors, created an interesting geometrical perspective that made the room appear much larger. Up to 1977 we manufactured single furniture pieces and interior constructions for and with Robert Haussmann.

How the Röthlisberger Kollektion Was Born

During the years of recession between 1975 and 1977, our volume of sales for Knoll International slumped enormously. Knoll, as a stock-listed enterprise, was taken over by the Italian Knoll producers who, logically enough, wanted to manufacture as much as possible in their own facilities. Within a short time we lost fifty percent of our turnover.

My father was able to make my sister and me aware of the problematics of the situation and to include us in the decision-making process of how to react to this crisis. I was 21 at the time, was a skilled carpenter and in the meantime had performed various jobs for my father. At the time, I had no big plans about stepping into the family business. But things turned out differently. My sister Ursula, who had completed her business training at Teo Jakob's, worked at Wohnbedarf Basel.

Our goal was clear: we wanted to get away from dependency on a bulk purchaser and, with our own production, get closer to, and deal more directly with, the market. In tandem with our friends, with Teo Jakob leading the way, the idea of our own furniture collection was discussed and developed. Prior to the Röthlisberger Kollektion, we produced the *Mondrian cabinets* from a Koni Ochsner design, which, starting in 1976, we successfully marketed in Switzerland and Germany.

We set up the goals and the guidelines of the Röthlisberger Kollektion that, for the most part, are still valid today. "We develop and manufacture furniture whose production is neither purely industrial nor purely artisanal. A product from the Röthlisberger Kollektion is situated between being handmade and factory-made. We do not want to hold the designers to any technical manufacturing specifications, but instead give them leeway to develop ways and solutions to transform a design into a finished product. A new product for the Röthlisberger Kollektion must be distinguishable from an already existing product."

In the summer of 1976, we invited Susi and Ueli Berger, Hans Eichenberger, Teo Jakob, Koni Ochsner, Robert and Trix Haussmann and Ueli Wieser to a visit in Gümligen and presented them with our ideas. All of them were enthusiastic. Under these above-noted guidelines, the Röthlisberger Kollektion was born. Teo Jakob and Ueli Wieser put together a wish-list of furniture for the first edition of the Röthlisberger Kollektion. To decide on the products, a jury was set up with Ernst Röthlisberger, Teo Jakob and Ueli Wieser. I was allowed to take down the minutes; my opinion was not in demand. When the jury decision was not clear and unanimous, we built the furniture anyway: the market was to be the final judge. At this time, I was working in the enterprise and was able to develop and fabricate selected prototypes. We developed 36 new pieces of furniture that in June 1977 were presented to select dealers and prospective buyers in Switzerland and Germany. The presentation was a complete success. The Röthlisberger Kollektion had survived its baptism of fire.

We launched new pieces of furniture, each within the framework of an edition. Thus in 1979 and in 1982 and from then on, we brought out an edition of eight to twelve new pieces every five years.

At the time I was only vaguely aware of how important this constellation was to become for my future life and my professional career. But suddenly everything became clear: I wanted to take over the company; I wanted to develop innovative furniture and I wanted to blaze new trails.

After completing my training with a degree as master carpenter, I joined my parent's company in 1981. In 1982 I assumed responsibility for the Röthlisberger Kollektion. We presented the 3rd edition and began exporting furniture to the U.S. Within a short period of time the Röthlisberger Kollektion was well known to insiders in Switzerland, Germany and America.

As of 1979 we, together with Trix and Robert Haussmann, produced many experiments involving artistically designed and handcrafted furniture. It was clear to me that these exclusive designs could not be compared to the normal furniture found in specialist shops and that they would have to be marketed in a different way.

With the collection /objekte/, in 1984 we launched an assortment of Haussmann's furniture pieces called *manierismo critico*, which we produced in a limited edition of 15 each: pillar stump, pillar cabinet, wall cabinet and bridge desk. All the pieces were made in grained olive-ash veneer and colour-coatings. Developing the details for these objects was extremely demanding, i.e., in their mechanical and handcrafted production that required a great deal of innovation, new techniques and a high degree of skilled craftsmanship.

As a result of this collaboration, I became better and better acquainted with Robert. Between the "distinguished gentleman from Zurich" and me, a close friendship evolved. Robert was a good teacher and mentor to me. Above all, he taught me that developing a product is not dependent on one person alone, but that close collaboration and the relationship between producer and designer make up the finished product. On the other hand, Robert sufficiently recognized the quality of my skills to appreciate and promote them.

In preparing for the 4th edition, Robert Haussmann, Hans Eichenberger, my father and I took a trip to Italy. We hoped to find inspiration from the great Italian manufacturers. We visited different furniture stores and makers of veneer. In one of the veneer factories we were given a look at the yellow-black striped tiger. We were all immediately enthusiastic about this special veneer that was made of natural wood but, through a new kind of industrial process, was given a new look. Robert named this tiger the "bastard". And I remarked: "If you design furniture with this 'bastard', we will manufacture it and adopt it into the Röthlisberger Kollektion." The hollow-profile table by Trix and Robert Haussmann and the curtain sideboard by Hans Eichenberger are the expression and the result of this trip to Italy.

Sägeweg 11 in Gümligen: Allgemeine Entwurfsanstalt
Because of the development and the success of the Röthlisberger Kollektion and because we increasingly carried out special interior installations, our workshop had become too small for us. In the summer of 2000 we were able to take over the

2002, New factory building
of Röthlisberger Schreinerei AG,
Gümligen. Architecture: by arb
Architekten Bern in collaboration
with Trix and Robert Haussmann.

premises of the Flückiger carpentry workshop at Sägeweg 11 in Gümligen. A new production site was to be built as quickly as possible. We made up a ground plan for the factory and worked out a service profile for the new building. I asked my friend Robert whether he would help me set up a profile of our requirements for the architects and if he would accept working on a jury. Robert replied to my request: he would be glad to be a member of the jury in assessing the factory building, but he would prefer to collaborate as architect and planner.

For the planning of our factory, we invited three architectural offices to participate in a competition. We were sent three outstanding designs which were all worthy of the award. arb Architects in Bern, together with Trix and Robert Haussmann, won the competition and were entrusted with the planning and execution of the new building. The decisive factor in favor of the arb Architects/Haussmann project was the straightforward, clear form, the absence of material and constructive experiments with their attendant risks and the clearly defined and verifiable costs.

Kurt Thut, Roland Keller and I were judge and jury; my father and Jürg Scheidegger advised us.

Our collaboration with the Haussmanns thus not only encompasses the design of furniture for the Röthlisberger Kollektion and interior installations. Trix and Robert Haussmann are also responsible for the aesthetics and the architecture of our factory building.

The Role of Alfred Hablützel

In connection with Robert, I often heard him speak of his friend Alfred Hablützel who was a self-taught graphic designer and photographer and in 1955 worked for Theo Jakob and who, with a stroke of the pen, deleted the "h" from Jakob's first name in the new logo.

It was he who also not only photographed Robert's first pieces of furniture, but in the following years also kept a critical eye on the designs created by others of his generation. Above all, he documented all the works of his friend Kurt Thut, for whom he, with his photographs, put together an exhibition in 2001.

Under Hablützel's direction, the *Forum kreativer Fabrikanten der Schweiz* was established in 1985, which presented itself at the Swiss furniture fairs as a quasi design center. He was also the initiator and curator of the exhibition *Mobilier Suisse.Création.Invention* at Centre Pompidou in Paris. For the later formation of *Forum 8*, he played midwife and active nursemaid in their exhibitions at Galerie Jamileh Weber in Zurich and at Kunsthalle Bern.

Hablützel always knew how to question our works critically and to hold a mirror up to us. His refreshing critique was and is always reliable. He puts his finger exactly on anything that is not in sync and, with his suggestions, knows how to stimulate us to greater deeds. At the end of 1995, I asked "Teddy" if he would help us in the selection and the development of new products. The 1997 and 2002 editions came about in collaboration. For over ten years, Hablützel was also responsible for the photography and public relations at the Röthlisberger Kollektion.

It is therefore natural that Hablützel – contemporary witness, protagonist, publicist and friend of Robert – is destined to be the right one to honour the work of Trix and Robert Haussmann.

Robert, many thanks for your friendship!
Peter Röthlisberger

From Wayside Encounter to Fellow Traveller

Extract from Kurt Thut's speech on March 20th 1992 at Teo Jakob's: "At the time I was in my last semester at the School of Applied Arts in Zurich. Hablützel had already left the School to earn his living (...). At the opening of the exhibition room – the first vernissage – we took Robert Haussmann with us to Teo Jakob's. We had admired him: he sat around in Select, smoked a pipe and read Stefan Zweig. Together with my furniture, we exhibited his string chairs and the table." The string chair was the first Haussmann piece that established troubling and, at the same time, fascinating opposition to my narrow standards and preferences for Bauhaus, Le Corbusier, Eames and other Americans. This chair, designed in 1953 as a semester assignment at the School of Applied Arts in Zurich, was the result of a theme set by Willy Guhl: a chair for the Museum Rietberg in Zurich. The fact that this design inspired me, a self-taught photographer, to one of my best photographs at the time and an award for the poster was due to its symbolic character. Robert Haussmann created his chair in harmony with the functional use and ethnologically handcrafted aspects of the task's requirements. The archetypical austerity of the 'Egyptian-esque' wooden construction and the spanned string that recalls a loom are fused to a markedly emblematic look. As an advocate of readable functions for furniture as well as for tools, I nonetheless still had some reservations vis-à-vis its symbolic character. It was in 1952 that Arne Jacobsen, under industrial conditions, designed the three-legged, plywood shell chair, which opened my eyes. Its likewise symbolic and associative shape obeys the technological as well as functional requirements and not the signal its name implies: ant. Convinced by the string chair, in my sales chats with doubting customers – after they had tried out the ant chair – I told them to sit on Robert's museum chair and test its ergonomic qualities: the narrow rectangular profiles of the wooden construction are only rounded at the edges where there is contact with body and leg. Probably Robert noticed as early as then that I might not only become a good photographer, but was already a good (idea)salesman ...

In 1955, Robert with his brother Peter opened the Haussmann & Haussmann (H & H) shop at Oberdorfstrasse 15 in Zurich. As with Teo Jakob in Bern, their access to collections like Knoll International with pieces by Mies van der Rohe, Florence Knoll and Eero Saarinen was blocked by suppliers who delivered exclusively to Wohnbedarf in Zurich. The underlying lack of really innovative upholstery furniture that could be integrat-ed into the existing range and was also commercially accessible led us at Teo Jakob's to begin looking around for ideas and designs by others. However I was met by designers of my generation with widespread skepticism and helplessness in the treatment of upholstery materials and techniques, especially those from the Guhl School. The exception was Robert Haussmann. Contrary to my bias against the over-upholstered, Robert – thanks to his experience at his father's tolerant workshop – had a craftsman's acute gift of observation. Despite this, one of H & H's first models awakened my suspicion yet again: the fauteuil that Robert designed in 1954 of flexible flat steel. As a purist, I judged it to be a recreation of Mies van der Rohe's *Barcelona Chair*. What always spoke against this was Haussmann's argument that his chair was collapsible. In Karl Mang's 1978 *History of Modern Furniture*, this upholstered chair is described as follows: "A chair newly developed from the ideas of Mies van der Rohe. Although Mies' designs were thought through to the last detail, they nevertheless allow positive transformations." In the *30 Year's of Teo Jakob* jubilee brochure published by Teo Jakob in 1983, he for the first time characterized Robert Haussmann's fauteuil as a homage to Mies van der Rohe.

After my first encounter with Robert in 1955 on the occasion of Teo Jakob's vernissage in his gallery room, the three black horses of Swiss furniture design met regularly: Hans Eichenberger, Robert Haussmann and Kurt Thut. Despite their differing but amiably tolerated standpoints on the process of designing, a creativity-inducing climate evolved that was in sync with aspects that Teo Jakob and I defined as to demand and salability. Within two years the three designers surprised us with interesting new chairs and tables, which also sold well. Based on planning commissions obtained by Hans Eichenberger and Robert Haussmann, several were designed for public space. The, in part, quite demanding constructions were fabricated in small series by dedicated craftsmen. As graphic designer, photographer, salesman and design critic, I was from the beginning of my employment at Teo Jakob's very conscious that by successful salesmanship I must earn all the freedom I enjoyed in configuring the product line and how it was to be portrayed. It was Hans Fischli, the director of the School of Applied Arts and Museum in Zurich, who was persuaded of the quality of these designs and showed an exhibition of our *neue metallmöbel* in the foyer of the Museum in the autumn of 1958. I still remember Robert's tongue-in-cheek remark when shown

1953, String chair with table (1955)
by Robert Haussmann

my poster design: "So, Teddy – I take it that the staggered sizes of the furniture photos correspond with your preferences." Robert knew exactly that I, as an ex-upholsterer, still have an allergic reaction to buttoned leather. Despite this, his chair found its way a month later into the Paris UNESCO office building in the Salle Suisse that he designed, where it received a more prominent place than on my poster.

The furniture exhibited in Zurich formed the startup line of the *swiss design* collection. I had won over Teo Jakob to offer these models as an international export collection in a high-end ambience yet more competitively priced by means of serial production instead of an expensive handcrafted fabrication.

For the first leaflets, I had drawn the *swiss design* signet with compass and T-square, influenced by a logo inscription for Hasselblad by Alfred Willimann that was never used. As a free-lance graphic designer and photographer, I was given the commission in 1963 to photograph 17 models – 13 of them by Robert Haussmann – of the expanded *swiss design* collection for an export catalogue. The photos were at the time an especially demanding challenge since they would be judged by the experienced New York importer, Charly Stendig. I like several

of the Haussmann models from that catalogue better today than I did then – a result of old-age sagacity or old-age mellowness? It wouldn't surprise me if one or the other of these fifty-year-old models were reissued. They testify, as do most of the designs by Trix and Robert Haussmann, to the disciplined way the two deal with the production processes of handcraftsmanship. Their vocabulary of forms has not evolved in imitation, but the more current functional forms of their new upholstered furniture are once again seen as authentic and meaningful. The Haussmann architects' unsentimental retro-references to, and the changed insights into, the function of furniture are part and parcel of the creative dialogue and the willingness to experiment, also in their collaboration with the Röthlisberger production.

With free-lance autonomy as my base, I also began a three-year stint with the magazine *interieur* of the Vereinigung Schweizer Innenarchitekten VSI (Swiss Interior Decorators Assoc.). For budgetary reasons of economy, I worked as editor, graphic designer and photographer in one and, along the way, learned by doing. There were three works by Robert that are today still compelling, which I published in *interieur*: in 1963,

Robert Haussmann was commissioned to design works for the Swiss national Expo 64. This included the interior decoration for the Centre de l'Hôtellerie. As part of these works, he created wooden chairs. In 1965 the theater in Ingolstadt/Danube commissioned Robert Haussmann, who designed a lighting system of prefabricated elements for the lobby of its new building. He not only succeeded in producing an additive geometry of light that was revolutionary in its versatility, but also in inventing an exposed-concrete architecture of glittering festiveness. And finally in the same year, the Zurich Kronenhalle bar is still today in its original state and has remained a much-quoted paragon and a "must" for Zurich's gastronomical scene.

In 1963 Robert met his future wife, Trix Högl. Ever since she completed her architectural studies at the ETH Zurich, they have worked together and have signed all their projects jointly. Since the beginning of the 1980s they have operated under the name of the Allgemeine Entwurfsanstalt or General Design Institute. In 1993, a new book, *Innenarchitektur in der Schweiz 1942–1992*, was published by the VSI for which Verena Huber and I did the graphic design and the editing and in which nine works by Trix and Robert Haussmann can be seen. One of which is the perhaps most spectacular space-modifying commission for Zurich's central railway station in 1992. Its unconventional spatial and technical interventions are testimony to their courage and maturity. On arrival, travelers find themselves quite unexpectedly immersed in the elegance of the Haussmann vocabulary of design and material, even in underground areas. An architectural calling card – instead of "Grüezi".

The 1966 founding of the advertising agency Hablützel & Jaquet h/j in Bern was the welcome occasion for me to hone my experience and my standards in judging product requirements, product functionality and product success. Via collaboration with the Dietiker chair factory in Stein am Rhein, both Robert Haussmann and I met its pragmatic CEO, Edlef Bandixen. As a photographer and advertiser, I for the first time was able, at close quarters within an industrial operation, to follow the background of what the disappointing market demand is for some product creations, but also the facts and the numbers behind the successful models. Included in these successes was the 3210 line designed by Robert Haussmann, one of the chairs on display at Expo 64 in Lausanne. The robust frame of this solid-wood chair with round legs and a cleverly formed narrow backrest has that certain something with which *the* chair differs from just any chair. In order to do justice to diverse us-

ages with very different requirements of comfort, appearance, durability and price, Robert Haussmann responded with a selection of variously worked seating surfaces: frames spanned in saddle leather, in strap- or string-weaves, frames inset with plywood, slats or a flat cushion. This comfortable chair subsequently proved capable of delighting its users in private dining rooms just as much as in restaurants. Thanks to its marked optical appearance, it triumphed as row seating not only in old and new churches, but also in community halls and meeting places. The series reached a production number of way over 100,000. In 1972, again for the Dietiker chair factory, Trix and Robert designed a chair system that received a silver medal from the American Institute of Business Designers.

In 1967 on Bern's 'house' mountain the Gurten, an unusual exhibition took place at the so-called *Chair-Fun* Auction. As a board member of the local Bern group of the Swiss Werkbund (SWB), I suggested this action as a way to fill its empty coffers. The point was to have chairs designed this time by artists instead of designers. At the time, the two professions were not considered identical. Among the artists who were invited and participated were, among others, Ueli Berger, Bernhard Luginbühl and Meret Oppenheim. Tired of the SWB's "staid formality", I, with subversive intent, let Trix and Robert Haussmann in Zurich in on the idea. They reacted, as I suspected, with great delight and created three masterly designed chair objects: the melting *Chocolate Chair*, three intertwined Thonet chairs in primary colours and the *Maso Chair*, a naked steel tube base frame for the plywood Eames' chair with five rubber buffers as a seat, with the perfidious addition of a pin cushion for spearing flower arrangements. The *Neon Chair*, made of fluorescent tubes and a seat pad covered in synthetic leopard fur, remained in Haussmann's home. From a present-day standpoint, what happened on the Gurten was, as it were, the first manifesto of postmodern furniture: a fusion of design and art, years before *Alchimia* and *Memphis*. I photographed the *Chocolate Chair* and the *Neon Chair* in 1970 with other artists' chair objects for the six-part poster series *De Sede is Latin for sitting* and a company portrait in mini format for the de Sede enterprise.

After de Sede, we at Hablützel & Jaquet gained another upholstery manufacturer as a client. According to my experience, advertisement in this case was the least of the problems; what was needed was fundamental briefing on running the business and creating the products. In a spontaneous tele-

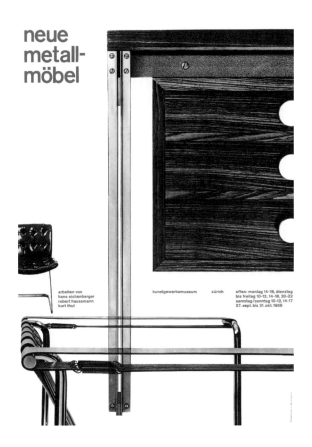

neue
metall-
möbel

arbeiten von
hans eichenberger
robert haussmann
kurt thut

kunstgewerbemuseum   zürich   offen: montag 14-18, dienstag
bis freitag 10-12, 14-18, 20-22
samstag/sonntag 10-12, 14-17
27. sept. bis 31. okt. 1958

phone conversation, I surprised the company head with a suggestion that he should employ me to get everything moving which we, from outside, could only recommend in exposés. It worked out as I imagined and, after 20 years in Bern, I vanished to the designer wilds of eastern Switzerland, to Wil, with my circle of friends seeing me off with doubtful looks and incredulous headshakes. As a trained upholsterer, I was once again to take up the subject which, 25 years ago, I believed I had left behind forever. At my few relaxing visits to the Haussmanns – always generously waiting for me with a bottle of Deutz champagne – I told them how I, equipped with a business card as a marketing director, grappled primarily and in sober realization with reducing a price list of over 850 models. And how, under the conditions that awaited me, I racked my brains to move closer to my ideas of a more up-to-date collection. Of course the fact did not escape me that Trix and Robert, with the examples of their *Working model I: furniture as an architectural quotation* which they showed me, enjoyed the luxury, so to speak, of an intellectual but also entertaining research project. That is, an occupation with furniture whose functional and optical modifications made them into costly treasures, produced in limited editions for customers who

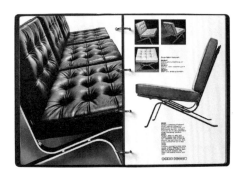
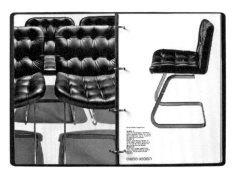
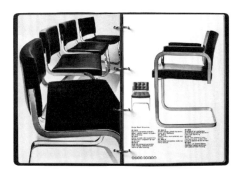

1958, Poster by Alfred Hablützel for the exhibition *neue metall-möbel* at the Museum of Design Zurich. Furniture by Hans Eichenberger, Robert Haussmann, Kurt Thut.

1963, First export catalogue of the *swiss design* collection. Examples of models by Robert Haussmann.

were just as enlightened as they were affluent. An engagement that was diametrically opposed to my problems: which was to create a new profile for a serial production, whose qualities needed to be measured by a price-performance ratio, i.e., both comfortable and affordable. With satisfaction I learned in 1977, via the press and the specialist trade, that the Röthlisberger Kollektion had produced roller-shutter cabinets in the Haussmanns' signature style that was familiar to me: a furniture program whose viability, constructive quality and look, but also its variability, is still today utterly convincing. After my insight into the mannerist experiments of Trix and Robert and in view of the louvered pieces, I wondered: is this still, once more, or simultaneously Haussmann?

With their research work *manierismo critico* and the upshot that questions the furniture's usefulness and appearance, their views on how to proceed in designing the Röthlisberger Kollektion have changed. Contrary to the seating furniture that, through the ergonomic requirements of mobility and technology, are much more related to those of a tool, cabinets and shelves, via their more passive use but also their widespread uniformity, are regarded by their owners with considerably less emotionality. For Trix and Robert this becomes a welcome invitation to design not only so as to fulfill usage requirements, but to invest in optically tangible refinements of construction and exterior finish. With their demand that the status and the presence of such furniture be activated within one's local surroundings, they found in Peter Röthlisberger an equally demanding entrepreneur, an experienced constructor and an unbiased discussion partner.

What in 1979 for me – again self-employed at Studio Hablützel – was quite unexpected and that made me for a long time a fellow traveler with the Haussmanns was a commission addressed to me, which resulted in a line that went by the name of *H-design for Mira-X*, a tale that would fill another book. It was Toni Cipolat, at the time the director of Möbel Pfister AG, founder and president of the governing board of the international Textilverlag Mira-X, who invited me to Suhr for a powwow. I had already worked as a photographer, graphic designer and copywriter advertising the Verner Panton collections. The subject of our talk was called: expanding the product line via a new textile theme. The revolutionary geometric-graphic patterns and the typical Panton colour range – not only in my eyes, but also expressed in slackened turnover – had passed its peak, and Mira-X urgently needed a new identification update for its fabrics. Already on the return trip from Suhr, it became clear to me that Trix and Robert were the right team for this project. In contrast to most of the architects, to them the concepts of decoration and ornament were not dirty words. I remember, for instance, the 'window dressing' that Robert Haussmann designed and had produced in 1969 at Zurich's School of Applied Arts during a teaching assignment; it was an interdisciplinary work in the interior-decorating class. Therefore the next day I called with the exciting news, and Robert fetched what he called his "favorite material", blanc de blanc, and set it to chill. I, as a converted federated artist-architect-builder and a fellow traveller, subsequently experienced the collaboration with Trix and Robert Haussmann for this one-of-a-kind, for Swiss conditions unique, commission as one that over several years was just as challenging as it was entertaining.

Today, 2011 – born a Scorpion like Robert in the same year – I am delighted that the Röthlisberger Kollektion on the occasion of Robert's 80th birthday has dedicated this book to his Design Institute.

Alfred Hablützel

1964, Detail of the Restaurant
Centre de l'Hôtellerie at
Expo 64. Interior decoration and
chairs by Robert Haussmann.

1964, Chair series 3210 by Robert
Haussmann for the Dietiker
chair factory. The polyvalence of
one and the same model sold over
100,000 copies.

1965, Lighting system made up of
modular elements by Robert
Haussmann. The theatre's new
building in Ingolstadt / Donau.
Published in *interieur* magazine.

1965, Bar at the Kronenhalle in
Zurich, designed and decorated by
Robert Haussmann with lighting
fixtures and table legs in brass by
the Giacometti brothers in Paris.

1967, *Chocolate Chair* and *Neon Chair* by Trix and Robert Haussmann, designed for *Chair-Fun* on the Gurten, Bern. In 1970 the same in a six part poster series for de Sede by Atelier Hablützel & Jaquet.

1972, Seating system by Trix and Robert Haussmann for the Dietiker chair factory. Awarded a silver medal by the American Institute of Business Designers.

Trix and Robert Haussmann
manierismo critico

Questioning the Dogma of Modernism

Under the working title of manierismo critico, *the architects Trix and Robert Haussmann have since the 1970s studied and planned (mental)architectural models. Their excursions to the classical Mannerism of the late Renaissance were meant to lead to an eventual update and reinterpretation of mannerist/illusionist style configurations. Several of the working models later became the prototypes for a limited object collection that was produced and sold at Röthlisberger's. The following article written by the Haussmanns was published with illustrations of their work in the journal* Werk, Bauen + Wohnen *on the theme of illusionism, No. 10/1981.*

Trix and Robert Haussmann: About Our Work

At the beginning of the 1970s, we again began to devote ourselves to the subject of Mannerism and illusionism. The quest to find other means of expression was the incentive, as well as our growing doubt in some of the modernist dogmas, a modernism whose increasing commercialization and internationalization, in our eyes, is guilty of complicity in the impoverishment of expression that has been gaining ground.

At that time, hardly anyone spoke of Mannerism in relation to contemporary architecture or to design. To be sure, at the latest after Gustav René Hocke's book, *Die Welt als Labyrinth*, 1957 *(The World as a Labyrinth)*, it was known that the concept could not be applied solely to the specific epochs of the 16th and 17th centuries, but was quite universal for all art movements that turn away from the rigidly classical or from classicism itself.

In contrast to modern painting and sculpture that have gone on to redevelop the mannerist heritage in many directions, modern architecture never gave it much thought. Its pioneers, in the battle against an ornamentation devoid of meaning and an increasingly superficial historicism, have thrown many means of expression overboard that had been practiced and handed-down for centuries. The purging process apparently requires this renunciation.

In any case, such illusionistic techniques had no place in "Neues Bauen". They would have been considered deceitful. Any ironic stance, also towards one's own work (a feature of almost all mannerists), would have anyway foundered on a modern sense of mission. And literary forms such as allegory, paraphrase, quotation, etc., would have been seen as blatant treason towards prevalent sentiments on modern construction. Also the mannerist concepts of the wondrous, the awe-some, the labyrinthine and the enigmatic had no place. Architecture had been denied the character of art, had been robbed of its irrational components as a result of the attempt to focus it exclusively on social and economic criteria.

Our excursion into the past made it soon clear to us that there is hardly anything new left to invent, but very much that needs to be reinterpreted and reformulated. In this context, we were first and foremost interested in the following design mediums:

- *defamiliarizing the material* by the free interpretation of a certain idea of material (illusion instead of imitation)
- *the creation of illusionary space through a reflecting surface.* Mirrors enable the optical "dissolution" of volumes, create infinite space, make spatial corrections, illusionary symmetries, etc.
- *the illusionistic transformation of mass or space by painterly means.* By applying any and every kind of perspective, and anamorphosis as a special form, working with contrasts such as light-dark, foreground-background, etc.
- *transforming the illusionistic mass or space by three-dimensional means.* Which includes constructed perspectives and anamorphoses
- *literary forms, metaphor, allegory, paraphrase, quotation,* the intention to create a relation to outside contents via the applied design mediums
- *complexity, ambiguity, multiple encoding,* a configuration that conveys statements at various levels and is thus "readable" in different ways
- *the incorporation of contradiction, turbulence, destruction,* the questioning of a work by its own stylist means.

We began to test several of these stylist means within the framework of small building projects in order to gain experience. With a more theoretical intent, we subsequently singled out individual themes in order to depict them in the clearest form possible. It was in this way that our so-called working models came about in the guise of objects. We chose the form of (mental)models because we didn't want to add yet another verbal manifesto to the many others. Our concern was to depict stylistic problems with the means of stylistic design itself; the model object, free of scale and motive, is especially suited for this.

We are thinking of continuing this series of working models. Others will have the problem of combining different

Trix and Robert Haussmann
indulge their appetite for
experimentation even at the dining
table in their apartment.

styles that will have the theme of anamorphosis and overlapping functions. The first of these "working models" followed by one example each from the field of architecture and product design are illustrated in the issue of *Werk, Bauen + Wohnen*, No. 10/1981.

All these works stem from an approach whose working title we call "critical Mannerism". This is neither a recipe nor a new design method that can do justice to all our objectives, but an attempt to rejuvenate lost tradition and give it a contemporary slant.

One of the essential starting points of mannerist design was and is to call into question habitual – and thus habit-formed – patterns of thinking and behaving. Mannerist meth-

ods are critical, even subversive, methods. They oppose any established concepts as to value and categorization, i.e., inflexibility of any kind. They are emancipating, a liberation also of humor, irony and, not least of all, self-irony.

As to illusionism as one segment of mannerist design, we must add that the deception is never meant in a deceitful sense. The viewer must be given the option to accept the invitation to capitalize on the illusion and to take his senses along for the ride.

This much on the conceptual background of our neo-mannerist experiments. We – as the educational products of Modernism – nonetheless know how difficult our attempt is to link a proven Modernism with historical tradition in a personal and future-oriented way without its being thrown into the soup pot of a diffuse Postmodernism.

Anyone who tries to revitalize old handicraft techniques must see the danger of slipping too close to kitsch. Yet despite this, we are more interested in the last master glasscutter who can cut facets than in the last snow leopard. (We think it is high time to found a kind of WWF for extinct handicraft professions.) A walk along a precipice includes the danger of a fall; it however allows a broad view of things.

Trix and Robert Haussmann

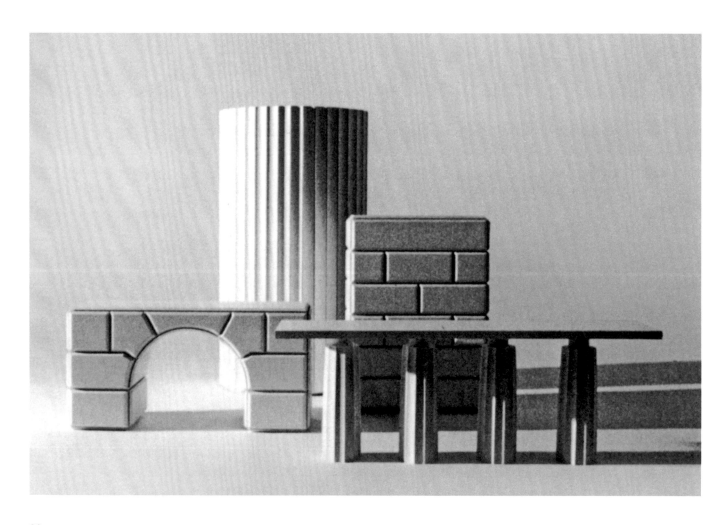

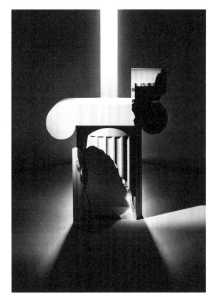

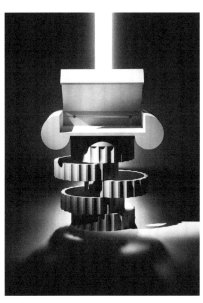
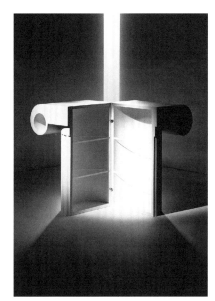

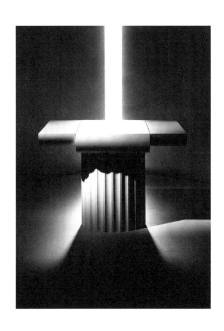

Left side: 1977, *Working Model I: Furniture as an Architectural Quotation.* Models made of Plexiglas and wood, painted white.

Right side: 1979, *Working Model V: Function Follows Form.* The metamorphosis of five pseudo-functional models of a given form. Made of Plexiglas and wood, painted white.

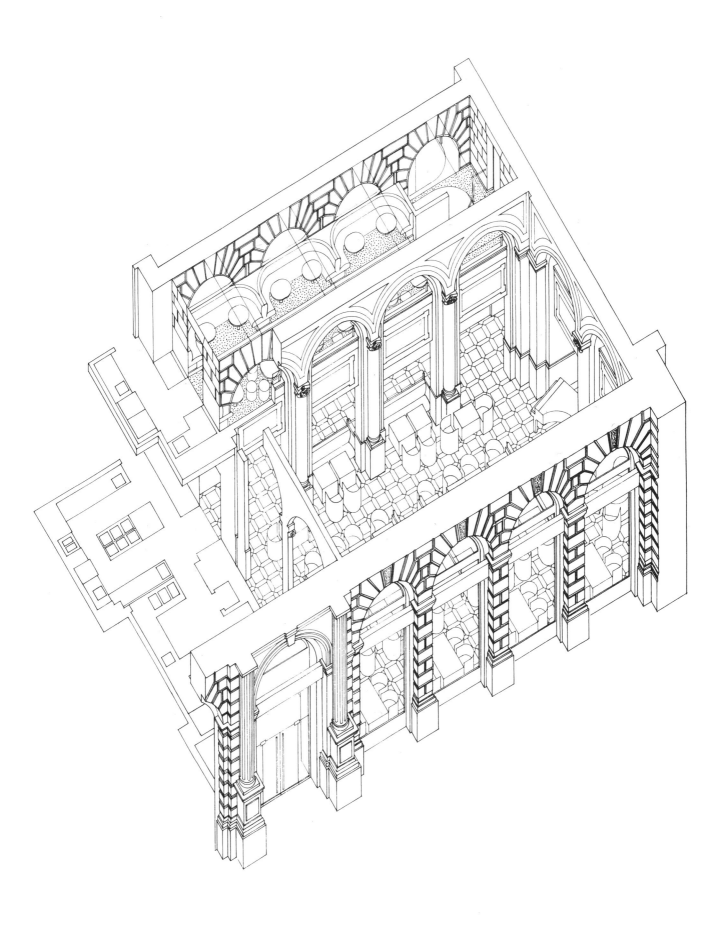

1980, Redesign of the Da Capo
restaurant and bar with
Stefan Zwicky in Zurich's main
train station. Example of a solution
for historical preservation by
means of illusionist painting.

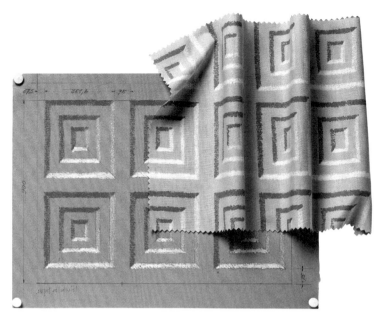

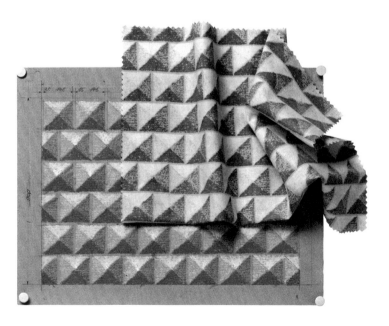

In 1981 Alfred Hablützel was commissioned by the international textile house Mira-X to develop new concepts for interior designed textiles. He decided on collaboration with Trix and Robert Haussmann. The trio designed several collections of printed and woven fabrics under the name *H-design for Mira-X*, partly citing Mannerist/illusionist design and allusions to historic motifs.

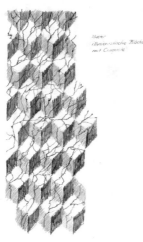

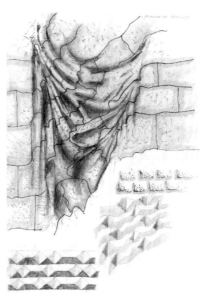

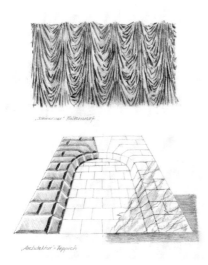

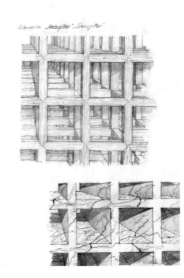

1981, Example from a series of sketches by Robert Haussmann for the potential design of rapport patterns and applications.

Working Model IX: Destruction as Ornament.

Top left: 1984, Destruction as motif in underglaze painting from a set of plates by Trix and Robert Hauss- mann for Swid & Powell New York.

Right: 1983, Destruction as the dec- orative, interlocked four por- tions of a square table. Model in Plexiglas, painted black and white.

Right side: Ironic destruction as wall decoration. Entrance area with «destructed» mirror glass at Hotel La Plaza in Basel designed by Trix and Robert Haussmann in 1985.

The years listed here refer to the year the Röthlisberger Kollektion first introduced the model. Any difference in reference to the year the models were designed is mentioned in the accompanying articles.

Trix and
Robert Haussmann

Furniture
Designs from
1977 onwards

Roller Shutters:
Outer Skin – Curtain – Façade

In correspondence with the idea and the requirements of Trix and Robert Haussmann, the Röthlisberger Manufacture experimented with finely wrought, solid, semi-round, wooden rods for an artfully louvered façade. Thanks to great flexibility and a correspondingly conceived shutter guide, the cabinet's all-round outer skin moves not only horizontally and vertically, but also opens and shuts in concave and convex curves – like a curtain.

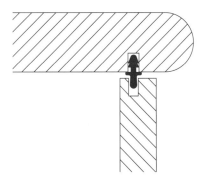

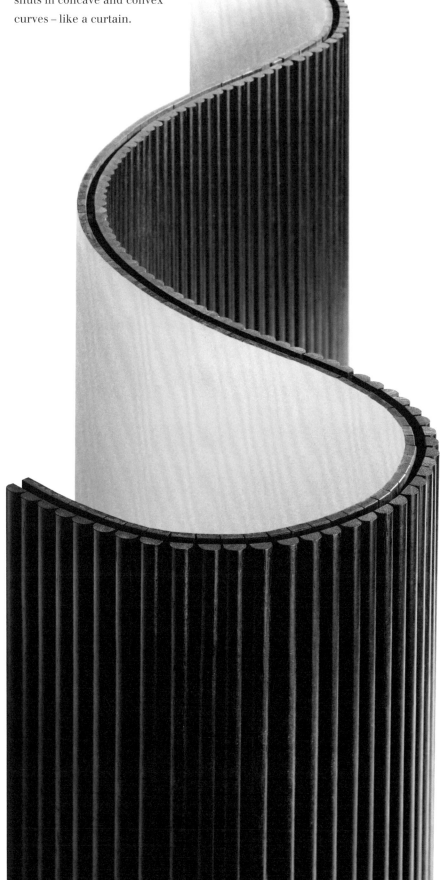

1977

Gracefulness and Functionality in One

The cabinets' A and B corpuses have a different base plan and are among the most thought-through contributors to the 1st edition of the Röthlisberger Kollektion. The units stacked one above the other – as space and purpose dictates – offer the visual pleasure of their fine grace and enduring delight in their use. And nothing has changed this since 1977, their year of birth.

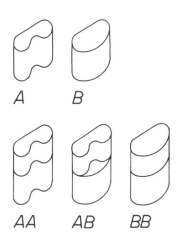

A   *B*

AA   *AB*   *BB*

Discover and Reinvent

In the 1977 roller shutter series, it is Trix and Robert Haussmann's process of search-and-find that equips the furniture with its old familiar as well as its updated functions, all under same, elegant mantle.

The quality of the designs up to today has been the benchmark of the standards and the demands that stands for the Röthlisberger Kollektion. The program encompasses: the rolltop secretary with a variety of

additions / the slim roller-shutter cabinets I that are three, two and one story high / the roller-shutter sideboard with a top in marble or granite.

1977

The Wall Cabinet
Working Model I: Furniture as an Architectural Quotation

This exemplar by the architects Trix and Robert Haussmann resulted from ther experiments and research into the disciplines of Mannerism and illusionism. The wall cabinet was a one-of-a-kind production. Röthlisberger presented it in a limited edition of 15 certified copies in monochrome paint and in grained olive-ash veneer. The architects' illusionist vocabulary also stamped the appearance of Zurich's 1977 boutique Lanvin as well as the *H-design* textile collection for *Mira-X* that they did in collaboration with Alfred Hablützel.

1979

The Bridge Desk
Working Model I: Furniture as an Architectural Quotation

At the same time as the wall desk, the duo created the bridge desk, whose stonework also surprisingly pulls out as drawers. For both prototypes, Robert Haussmann tried his skill at the old technique of marbling. The bridge desk is part of the object collection that Röthlisberger produced in a limited edition in monochrome paint and grained olive-ash veneer. In 1980 the architects Trix and Robert Haussmann thoroughly did over the Da Capo restaurant at Zurich's central railway station: a spectacular, illusionistically designed bar on the mezzanine floor with elements translocated from the outside façade.

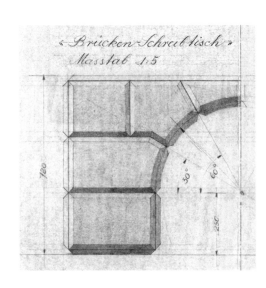

The Experience: Less Is More

In 1978 Trix and Robert Haussmann designed the three pieces of furniture with end-grain inlays carried out by the carpenter Dumeng Raffainer in Zurich, inspired by *Working Model III: Ornament Disrupts the Form.* In the manner of a trompe-l'oeil, the ornamentation across the table's corner from a 1st century B.C. Antioch floor mosaic was given new life. In a dialogue with their senior partner, Ernst Röthlisberger, Trix and Robert Haussmann complied with his wish to spread the "disruptive" inlay across the whole surface of the furniture. The ingenious intellectual interpretation of the "less is more" dictate was transformed into a compromise that became a much-admired work of meticulous tenacity. What was new for the craftsmen at Röthlisberger was fabricating the inlaid ornaments from puzzle bits by means of the same sawing technique used in the 15th century.

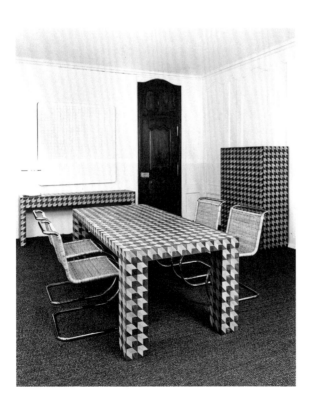

1979

40

Object – Edifice – Furniture
Working Model IV: Seven Codes

The 1978 mirror wardrobe *Seven Codes* that Trix and Robert Haussmann designed as *Working Model IV* is an object that is a portent of the multiple ways to read the Mannerist/illusionist intention of its designers. The work is a masterpiece vis-à-vis the complexity of its conception as well as vis-à-vis its artisanal skill. It can be considered the quintessence of several years of research and project work on *manierismo critico*. The thrice-knotted cloth was carefully sketched by Dumeng Raffainer in Zurich and then meticulously copied in solid wood inlay by Röthlisberger craftsmen, who then integrated the whole into the ingrained mirror surfaces. One of the two produced representative pieces stands in Landesmuseum Zurich. Its draped cloth in lead glazing was hung from the portal of the Passage Galleria in Hamburg that the architects designed in 1983.

The Pillar Stump
Working Model II: Function Disrupts Form

With the idea of *Working Model II* defined as a disruption – in an ironic reversal of the thesis repeated ad nauseam of "form follows function" – Trix and Robert Haussmann succeeded in creating their arguably most spectacular furniture object. Their idea of segmenting the stump of a pillar into eleven flat cylinders and swinging them out from a vertical and sideways-shifted axis as containers with glass bottoms was a welcome constructional assignment for senior partner Ernst Röthlisberger. Like the wall cabinet and the bridge desk, this third working model in the object collection is in a limited edition of 15 certified copies.

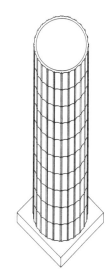
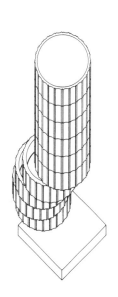
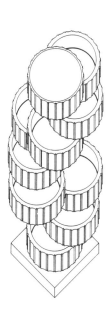
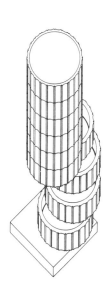

Delight in How an Aesthetical Disruption Functions

The fascination with the almost unlimited possibilities for modifying the pillar stump induced the Haussmann duo to introduce the optical phenomenon of their object into other fields of their work and give it other functions. For instance in 1980 on Zurich's Bahnhof-strasse with the interior decoration for the Weinberg fashion house, realized as mannerist stage architecture. In 1984, Peter Röthlisberger was asked to create an exclusive furniture object for the German furniture store for their upcoming company jubilee. A fabrication of 110 miniature pillar stumps on a scale of 1 to 5 was agreed on. This small treasure from Gümligen found worldwide, enthusiastic owners who took pleasure in Haussmann's function-disrupting form.

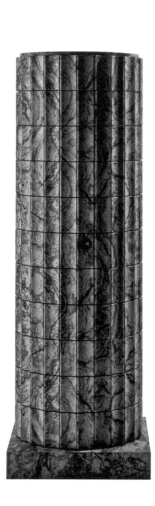

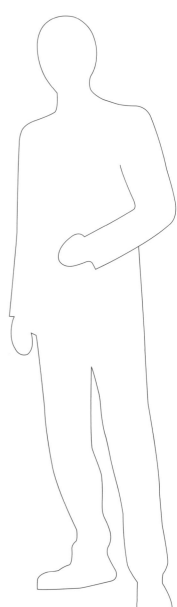

1982

How the Campari Bottle Helps in Finding a Form

For the 3rd edition of the 1982 Röthlisberger Kollektion, Trix and Robert Haussmann designed the pallet rack. Contrary to widespread opinion, this piece is not a nostalgic reference to the 1950s. It is the result of the complex process of carrying out a user-friendly idea: a shelf construction in the geometric forms of circle and square with stacked shelves and four steel tube supports. A freestanding piece with practical uses. Experience proved, however, that with the desired diameter and the spacing between the racks, quick and comfortable access was only to things set on the edges. The Haussmanns responded to this drawback with a meaningfully placed cutout of the circular panels. The form that emerged – similar to an artist's palette – is turned 90° clockwise at each level. Each rack is hereby supported at three points by the vertically-set steel tubes. With this designer operation, each level offers a rack that is both open above and more accessible. In this way there is room enough to set down a tall bottle of Campari.

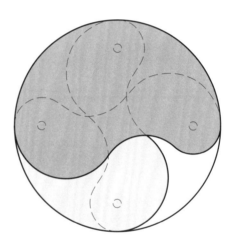

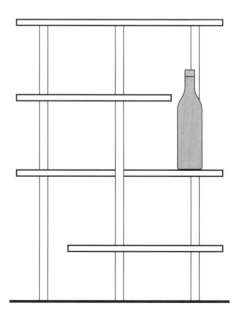

Daring Transformation

The Haussmanns' last (in 1977) designed columnar cabinet as *Furniture as an Architectural Quotation* has figured since 1984 in the Röthlisberger object collection. Trix and Robert Haussmann's architecture office, which since 1981 has operated under the name Allgemeine Entwurfsanstalt in order to deliberately avoid a commitment to any one field of design, subsequently and surprisingly transferred its design philosophy and leitmotif into another product field within architecture's entourage: namely, the interior decorating creation of textiles, e.g., *H-design for Mira-X* in 1980 together with Alfred Hablützel. With the *Ligneus* fabrics, their intention was to distort and dematerialize the character of wood and textiles. The forefather of this transformation was the pillar stump cabinet. The fluting and the lively character of grained olive ash provided the wherewithal for a daring and successful transfer – onto velvet and silk.

Dealing with Block Stripes

In the beginning it was silk chiffon with black-and-white block stripes that Robert Haussmann spread out on the table to show his photographer friend and with both hands cautiously bunched it together into sculptural folds and requested a photograph: the proper assignment for Alfred Hablützel, trained upholsterer and decorator. The Allgemeine Entwurfsanstalt knew how to handle the result. In 1984, a set of plates came about that they designed for Swid & Powell in New York. In 1988, Abet Print fabricated a synthetic resin panel for a Trix-and-Haussmann designed sideboard, completely sheathed with the same motif in a postforming process for the Wogg Collection. Peter Röthlisberger could hardly hide the envy he felt vis-à-vis his friendly rivals at Wogg's, Otto and Willi Gläser, for this very successful design. (Lower photo by Christian Kurz from *Das Magazin*, No. 24/1989)

1984

52

Manhattan Kindles Associations and Conversations

To the architects Trix and Robert Haussmann, block stripes – flat or in motion and since their experiments with *manierismo critico* – are part and parcel of the much varied design motif of surfaces. The example of the urban furniture series *Manhattan* from 1987 with its impressive horizontal stripes kindles memories of Siena. With this architecturesque *Manhattan* group, it is not Tuscan marble but light and dark stripes in grained veneer that cover the cabinets' outer skin. Which is why they can all be placed independently in the room. The Haussmann's elegant building-block furniture will possibly lead architectural connoisseurs to discuss Adolf Loos, whose 1927 design of a striped house for Josephine Baker in Paris was meant as a homage but never built. (Photo by Alfred Hablützel with Trix and Robert Haussmann from the *Schweizer Illustrierte* of 2 Nov 1987)

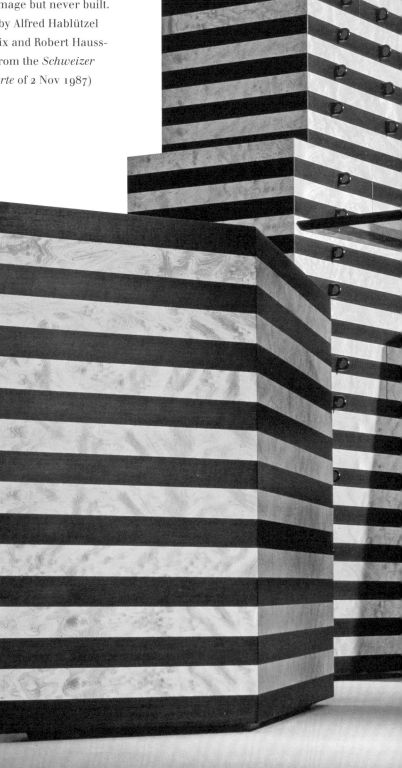

54

Manhattan Cabinets Love to Be Handled

Trix and Robert Hauss-mann's *Manhattan* cabinets harbor surprisingly handy and diverse practical uses. The stackable chests of drawers can be placed individually, in twos or threes, one above the other.

The wedge-shaped bar was described in one brochure of the Röthlisberger Kol-lektion as a "skyscraper for highpotency drinks". When a *Manhattan* cocktail is served, a countertop can be folded out from the interior

with a single gesture. The Haussmann's corner secretary reminds us of the practical function of furniture designed for corners long before Mod-ernism.

1987

Material over Function

In 1986, Peter Röthlisberger discovered at an Italian manufacturer's an unusual, yellow-black moiré pattern called tiger veneer. At fabrication, the dyed material is pressed into a thick, rippled sandwich. The following horizontal cut of a wooden board layered in this way provides new veneer with a tiger-patterned grain: synthetic wood out of wood. Confronted with this blatantly expressive material, Peter Röthlisberger with the designer Hans Eichenberger and the two Haussmanns agreed to set the application of this patterned surface at the start of a new furniture design. This actual reversal of what the school of thought considers the proper chronology for the designing process actually proved to stimulate fresh ideas. Hans Eichen-berger took a forgotten sideboard closed with a curtain as an example. Trix and Robert Haussmann used the outer surface material to make a hollow body ingeniously consisting of nine planes – the hollow section table.

1987

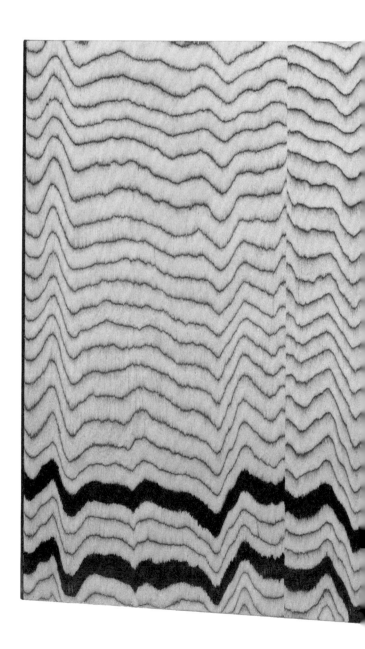

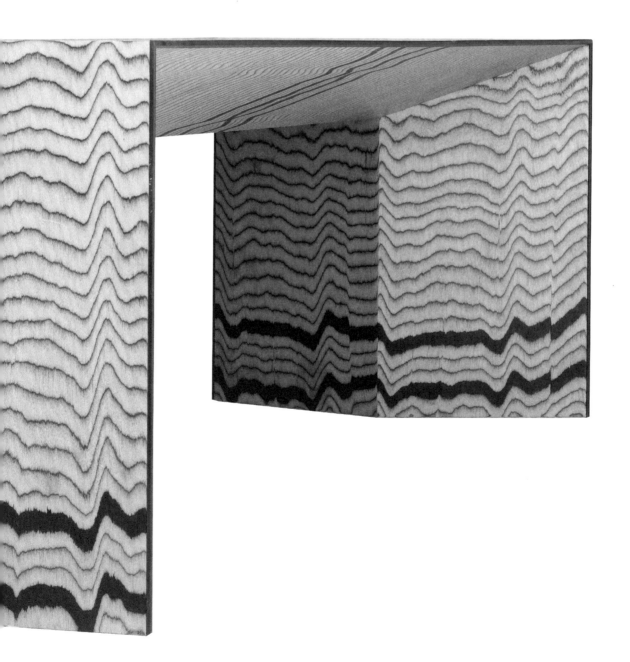

Open Sesame

In the 1990s the overcrowd-
ed electronic landscapes
in our living rooms urgently
demanded a compact and
screened-off storage space.
Trix and Robert Haussmann
responded with their ar-
moire tower *Sesame*, intelli-
gently crafted to protect
precious hi-fi components.
The name *Sesame* pledges a
certain magic, which is
instantly fulfilled by the
soundless opening of
the shield-like doors at the
touch of a finger or a re-
mote. The way the almost
invisible fittings amaz-
ingly allow both doors to
glide to the mirrored
sides of the tower astounds
users.

1990

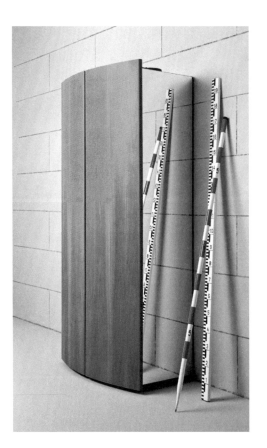
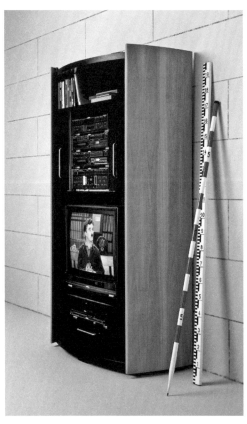

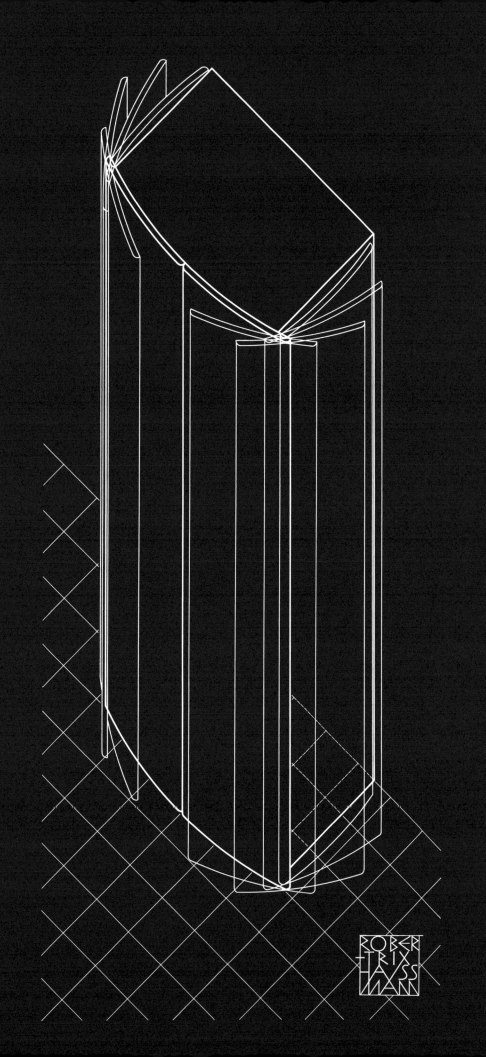

Torre – a Geometric Challenge

This fascinatingly changing geometry is a visual pleasure provided by the cubic grid of Trix and Robert Haussmann, who designed it in response to a welcome stylistic commission. For the 1980 design for illusionistic inlay on sliding doors, they set the perspectival vanishing point at the right upper corner of the square. In 1991 the impulse to design the *Torre* object came from the Weissenhof Institute of the Stuttgart State Academy of Art and Design for its exhibition and book project "Erbstücke" (Heirlooms). The designers Trix and Robert Haussmann were invited to submit a work. One of the project sponsors from industry and craftwork was Peter Röthlisberger. The design *Torre* required knowhow from the architects and perseverance from the craftsmen to an almost unprecedented extent. This two-door free-standing armoire seems to viewers to present an openwork grid, but in reality is an all-round trompe-l'oeil on a two-dimensional plane. To obtain this illusion with its light and shadow effects, the artisans worked with the natural tones of maple, beech, pear tree and walnut veneer. The see-through illusion is achieved with level, ingrained mirrors. Even the pencil for the signature is inlaid. Till today only 9 exemplars have been made to order, hardly surprising, since each one demands 350 hours of the precise hand, the sharp eye and the mental concentration of the carpenter.

1991

Volumes Mirrored Out – Room Mirrored In

With their love of jack-in-the-box surprises, Trix and Robert Haussmann have used mirrors as an indispensable medium in their design arsenal. In contrast to the decorative uses of conventional interior decorating, the mirror assumes a calculated function in their works. As already with their *Sesame* tower (pages 60/61), the three spacious cabinets designed in 1991 have mirrored sides. Here you experience the artistic intention behind the mirrors in their virtual double function: volumes mirrored out – room mirrored in.

1991

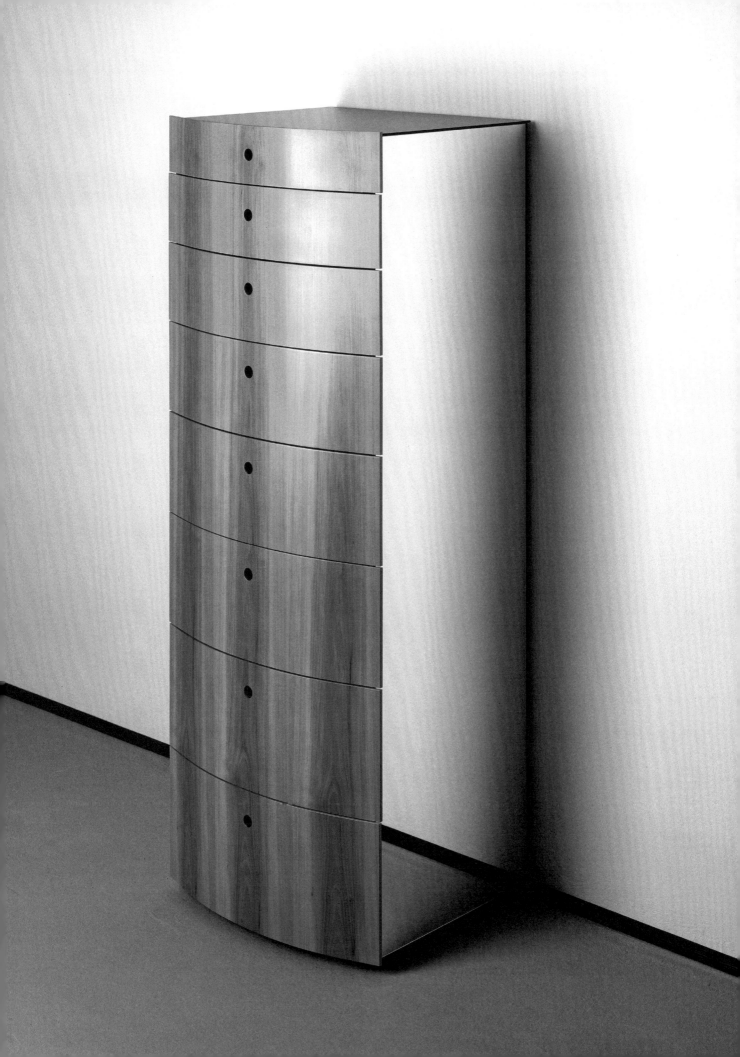

Trias – The Art of Joining

The tripod designed by Trix and Robert Haussmann in 1992 on which glass and wooden tabletops rest, were produced by Röthlisberger carpenters as their Gordian knot. Unexpectedly they succeeded in joining three beech wood spars, with identical grooves of twelve cuts each, firmly together in one process and, to be on the safe side, also with glue. In the ensemble seen here, it once again proves how furniture designs from different periods harmonize in the Röthlisberger Kol-lektion without any generational friction. Displayed on the carpet by Clara Saal and Alfred Hablützel from the *Caro Block* Collection, 1992: the chair by Willy Guhl (Robert Haussmann's teacher), designed in 1943 and available in the Röthlisberger Kollektion since 2002, seen here in the company of a *Trias* table. On the wall: the sideboard by Trix and Robert Haussmann from the 1977 1st edition of the Röthlisberger Kollektion.

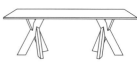

1992

Disconcert via Artifice

It is a feature of their talent that Trix and Robert Haussmann can make the design of simple things not too simple. They also succeeded in doing this in 1992 with *Janus*. Besides the utilitarian purpose of these freestanding shelves that allow access from both sides, it is only at a closer look that you notice a further optical quality. The shelves surprise and disconcert you by their various aspects. Seen on the one side as a slim shelf of thin boards, from the other side and from the same perspective, it looks like a considerably more robust shelf construction. The non-essential artifice shows us how, with the design's more problematic requirements, making a quite simple shelve unit can be a technical production challenge.

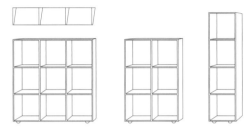

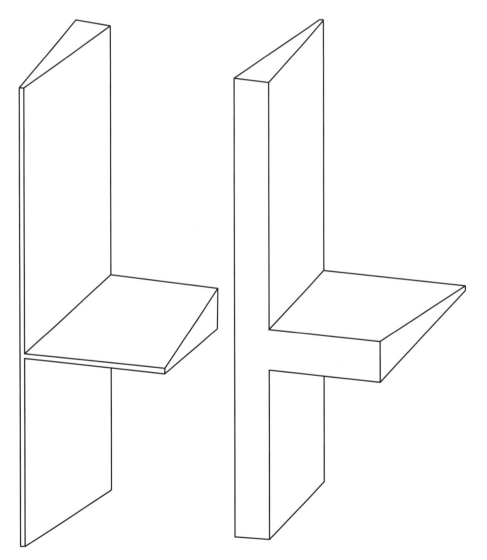

Cabinet Front as Picture Plane

In the history of cabinet units, we can read emotional reactions similar to those expressed about the façades of buildings. Peter Röthlisberger remembers how, after a mutual visit to the Rothko exhibition in Zurich, the discussion with the two Haussmanns centered on the mundane uniformity of modern furniture frontage. Trix and Robert Haussmann had already responded with colored sketches. Their idea to recognizably signal the variation in the volumes behind the drawers and door fronts was convincing. The painterly style of some natural root-grained veneer discovered at Röthlisberger's provided the desired look for the exterior surfaces. The three 1993 designs, baptized *Color* with rhythmically arranged fronts, operate in the room as both furniture and mobile picture planes.

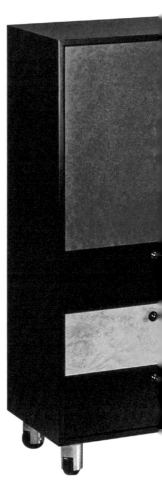

1993

Jeux des Panneaux – How to Play Them

It was a patented bonding procedure for a magnetic slideway, developed by Peter Röthlisberger, that inspired and occupied Trix and Robert Haussmann in 2000 at the beginning of a work. Their three, four or five story shelf *Jeux des Panneaux* has been constructed along the lines of the bonding pattern of ashlar masonry. It creates recessed niches closed partially by sliding doors. As whim and need take you, the position of the gliding "panneaux" of mirror glass or other materials can be varied horizontally. How does this happen with no rails or metal fittings in sight? The secret lies in a thin invisible steel band under the veneer of the horizontal board's front edge. It is a magnetic slideway that operates by grace of the magnets mounted behind the "panneaux". Their adhesive capability is apportioned in such a way that the "panneaux" can be as easily slid open-closed as relocated.

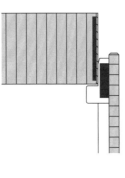

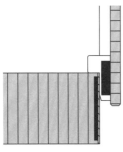

2002

The Candidness of a Computer-Controlled Vocabulary of Forms

The history of the way furniture was developed runs parallel to the history of the way the materials, technologies and tools developed in their use. Still today, the sum of these aspects is what primarily determines the form. The switch from an analog to a digital era also at Röthlisberger's presents a new creative challenge. With the models *Credenza*, Trix and Robert Haussmann, together with the technicians at Röthlisberger's, took up this challenge. Contrary to archetypal massive cabinets, they designed the fronts with a clever wavy relief of unmistakably solid wood. However, such work was not the result of weeks of a carpenter's hard labor but the result via the formal vocabulary of an ingeniously programmed, computer-controlled automaton. A new candidness. It is striking that the insides of the doors fused from five panels are missing the otherwise necessary traditional crossbars fitted with a wooden clamp. In their place the crossbars are flush with the doors and contribute to their stability. They are firmly bound only to the two outer vertical panels. For which reason the solid wood's natural traverse forces – that vary according to temperature and humidity – are only effective within the fixed width of the door. Peter Röthlisberger patented this technique, which is similar to that of a door construction made from frame and filling.

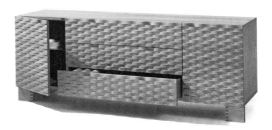

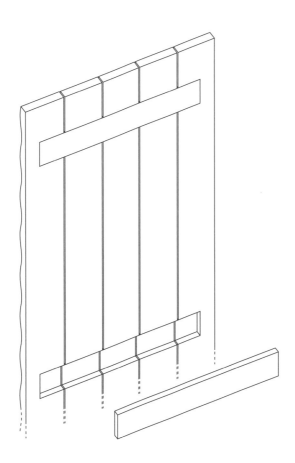

2007

74

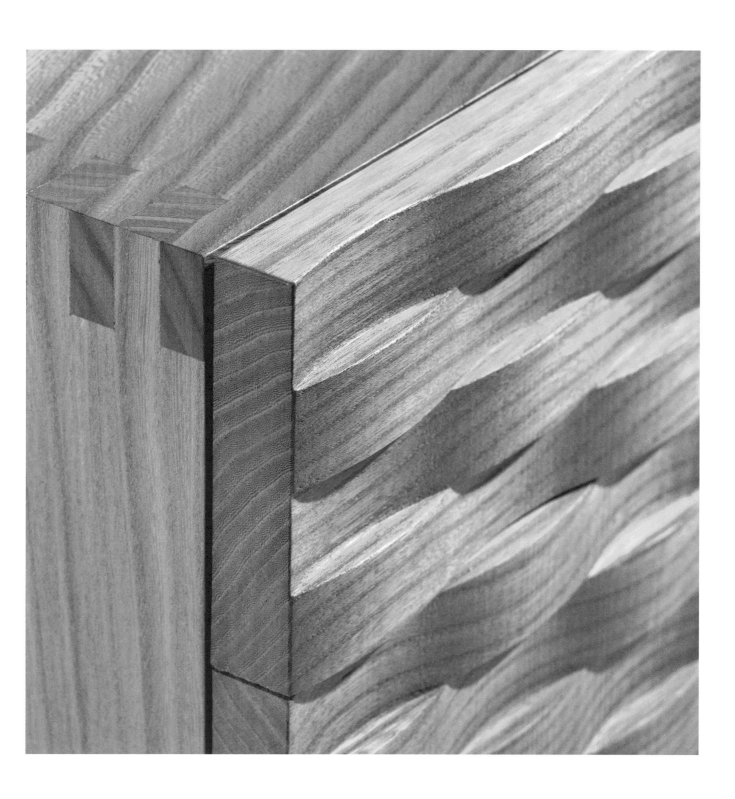

Biographies of Trix and Robert Haussmann

Robert Haussmann

Robert Haussmann studied in Zurich and Amsterdam. After several years of practical experience in the building industry, he has since 1956 been self-employed. From 1972 to 1978 Robert Haussmann taught interior decoration and product design at the University of the Arts in Zurich. From 1979 to 1981 he was guest lecturer for architectural design at ETH in Zurich and from 1986 to 1998 Professor for architectural design at the Stuttgart State Academy of Art and Design.

Trix Haussmann-Högl

Trix Haussmann-Högl studied at ETH in Zurich. After her degree in architecture, she finished her postgraduate studies at the Eidgenössische Institut für Orts-, Regional- und Landesplanung ORL in Zurich. Trix Haussmann was from 1997 to 2002 a lecturer at ETH in Zurich.

Allgemeine Entwurfsanstalt

Since 1967 Trix and Robert Haussmann have worked in tandem at their architecture and design office. Since 1981 they have operated in Zurich under the name of Allgemeine Entwurfsanstalt. Their practice ranges from the planning, building and renovation in private, business and public fields to the product design for clients at home and abroad.

Top: Robert and Trix Haussmann
Bottom: Robert Haussmann

Robert and Trix Haussmann

Alfred Hablützel, Trix and Robert Haussmann

Top: Trix Haussmann
Bottom: Robert Haussmann

Top: Willy Guhl (first from left),
Robert Haussmann (third from left),
Alfred Hablützel (fifth from left)
Middle: Alfred Hablützel, Robert Haussmann,
Eleonora Riva-Peduzzi, Trix Haussmann
Bottom: Benedikt Loderer, Robert Haussmann

Top: Robert Haussmann, Peter Röthlisberger
Middle: Hans Eichenberger, Ubald Klug,
Alfred Hablützel, Robert Haussmann
Bottom: Robert and Trix Haussmann

Trix Haussmann and Alfred Hablützel

Both photographs: Trix and Robert Haussmann

Photo Credits, Publishing Information

Photo Credits

Archive Hablützel	pages 76, 77
Archive Haussmann	pages 19, 25, 38, 39, 61, 62 left, 69, 76, 77
Archive *interieur* 3/1966	page 14 top
Archive Röthlisberger	pages 44, 45, 46, 76, 77
Alain Bucher	pages 6, 72, 74, 75
Alain Bucher/Alfred Hablützel	pages 29, 30, 34/35, 37, 41, 66, 73
Matthias Buser	page 20
Sabine Dreher	page 77 (colour photograph)
Alfred Hablützel	pages 9, 11, 13, 15 top, 17, 23, 24, 27, 36 right, 40 bottom, 43, 47, 50, 51, 53, 54/55, 56, 58, 59, 60, 64, 65, 71
Trix Haussmann	page 42
Kai Loges	pages 62 right, 63
Marco Schibig	pages 57, 70
Fred Waldvogel	pages 14 bottom, 15 bottom, 21, 26, 31, 32, 33, 36 lower left, 36 upper left, 40 top, 52 top
Masato Yokoyama	page 67

List of Sources

pages 17, 23 bottom, 54	Museum of Design, Design Collection, Zurich University of the Arts permanent loan of the Swiss Federation, Bundesamt für Kultur

Publishing Information

Editor	Röthlisberger Kollektion, Gümligen
Concept	Alfred Hablützel, Thomas Petraschke
Editorial Work, Photo Selection	Alfred Hablützel
Editing	Jonas Hablützel
English Translation	Jeanne Haunschild
Graphic Design	Flux Design, Heidi Windlin, Basel
Lithography	LAC AG, Basel
Production	Stämpfli Publikationen AG, Bern
Paper	Nettuno, Lessebo Smooth White
Font	Helvetica, Walbaum

n'li

© 2011 by Verlag Niggli AG, Sulgen | Zürich, www.niggli.ch
ISBN 978-3-7212-0818-4: English Edition
ISBN 978-3-7212-0817-7: German Edition
ISBN 978-3-7212-0819-1: French Edition